MAGIC PAINT
WITH
BRIAN CLARKE

Stained Glass

"Art has been the great passion of my life:
a magnificent adventure. I hope this book
sparks your creativity and helps you
to find the joy and magic in art."

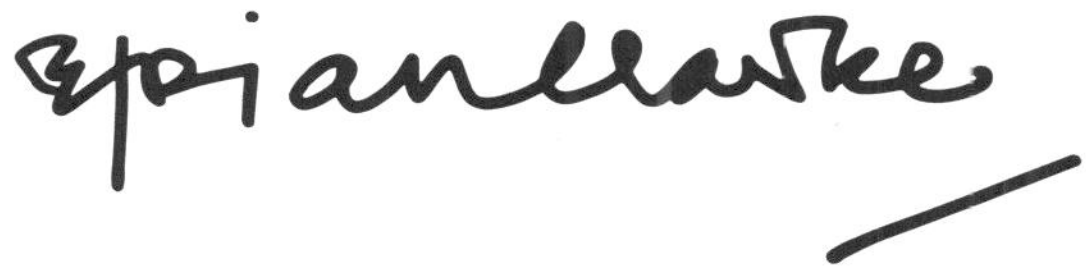

HENI Publishing, London

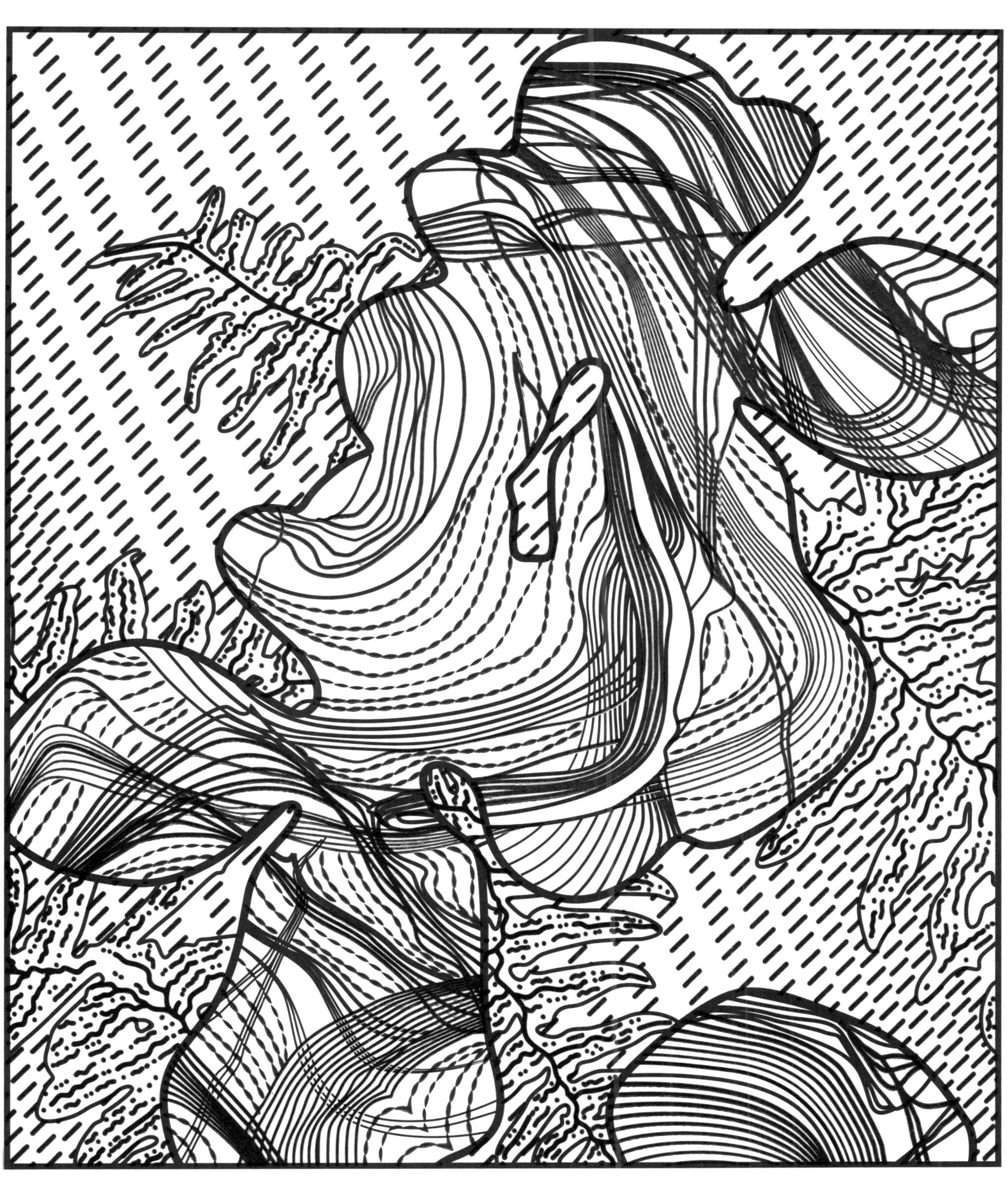

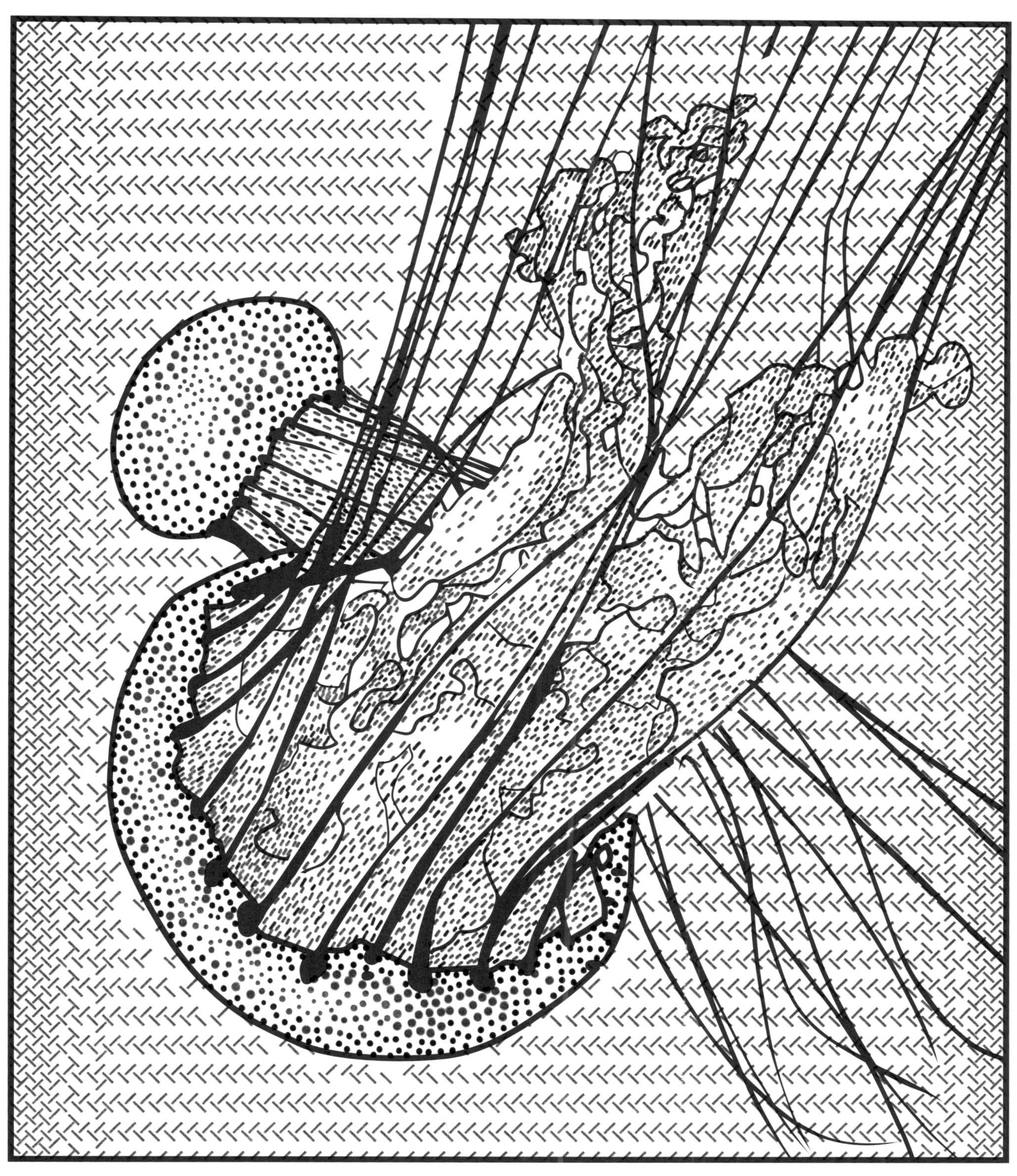

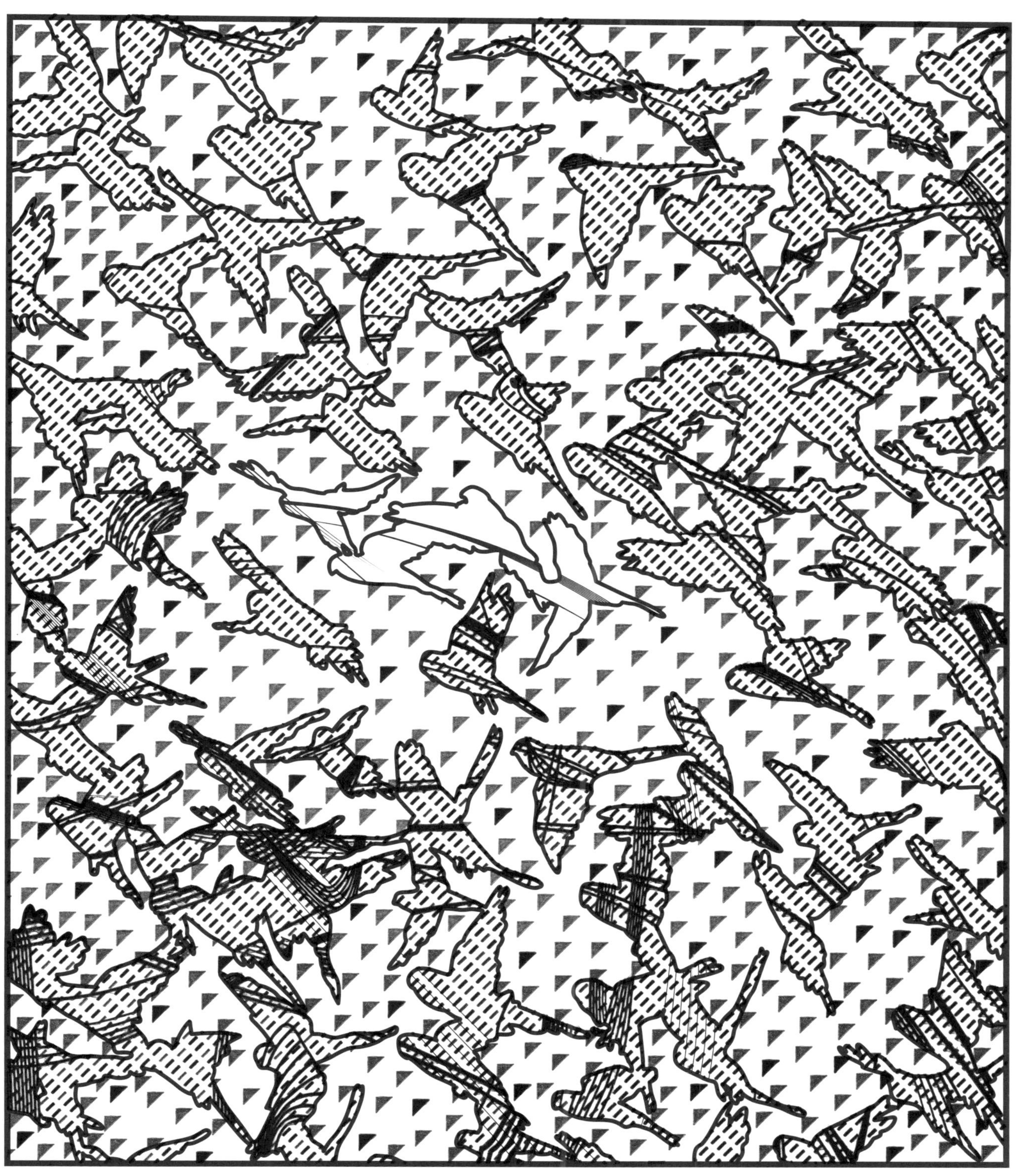

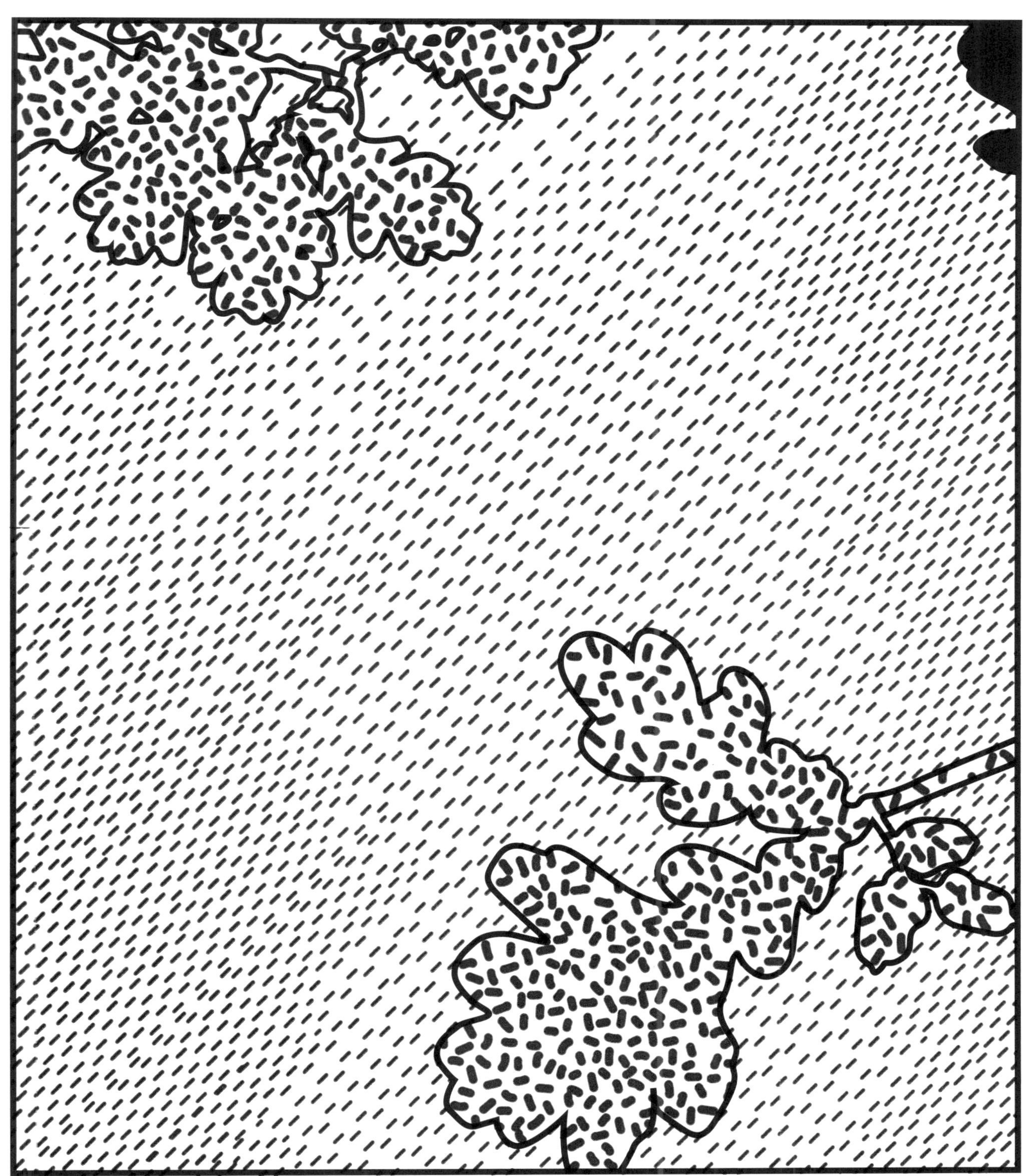

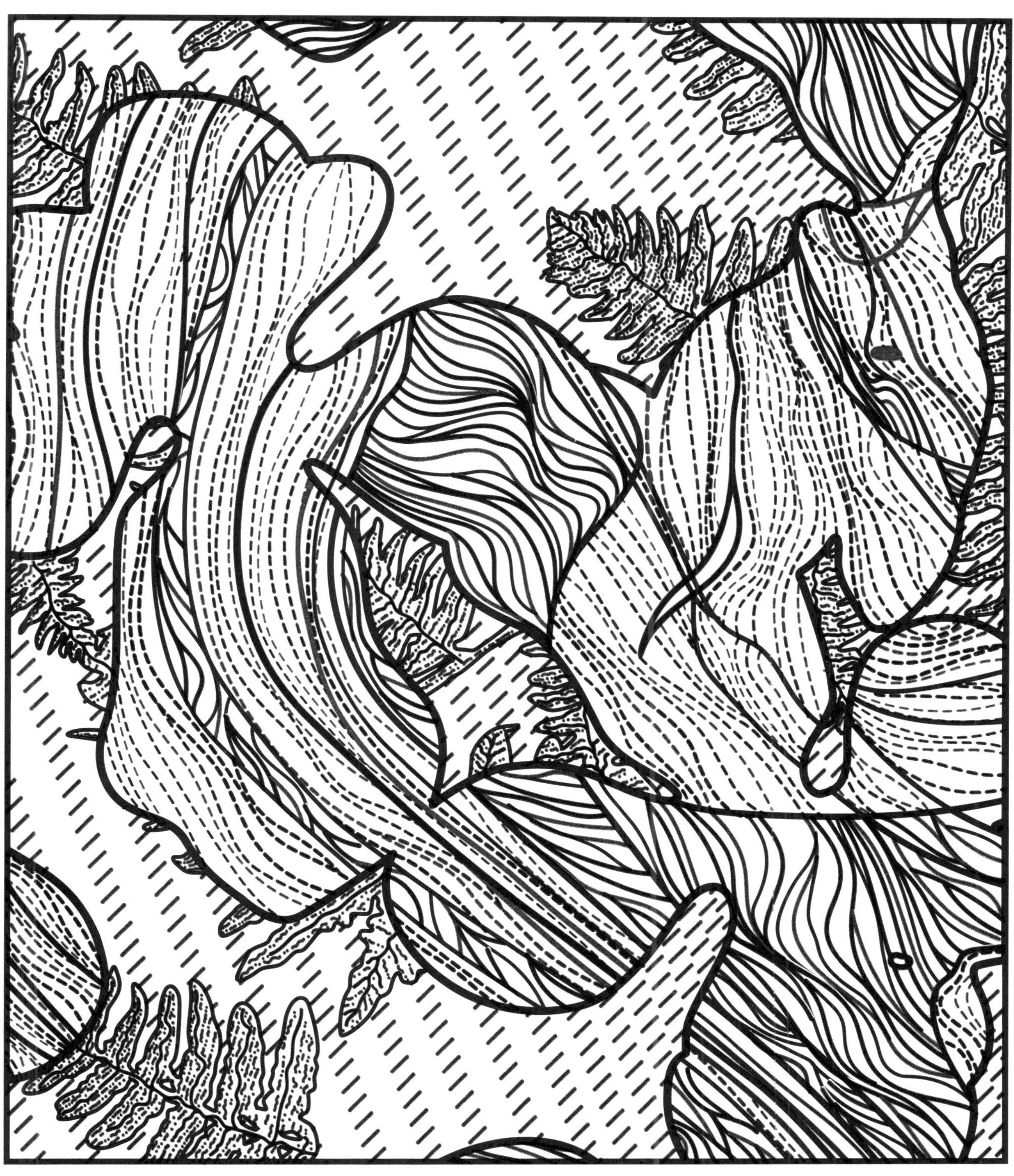

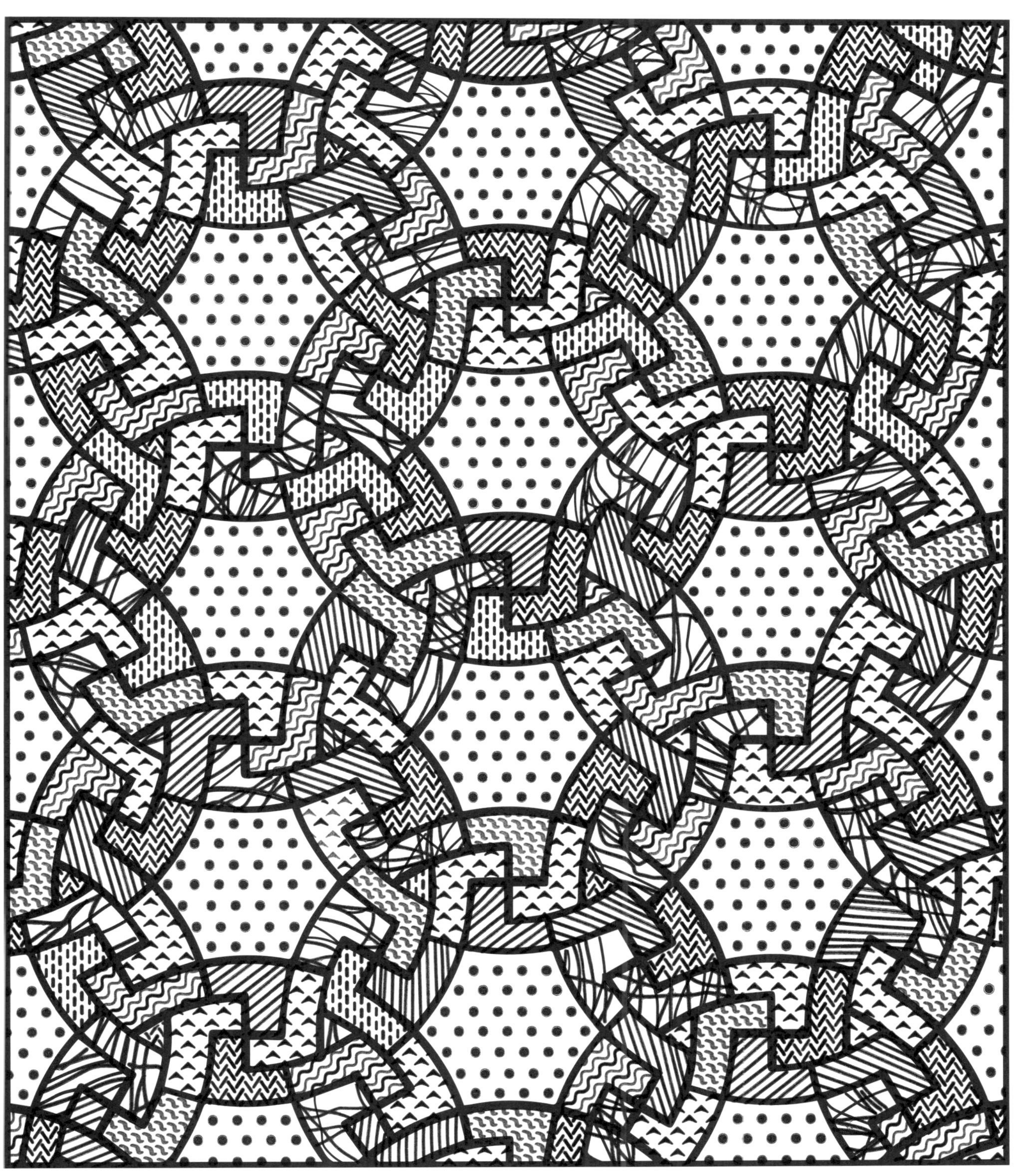

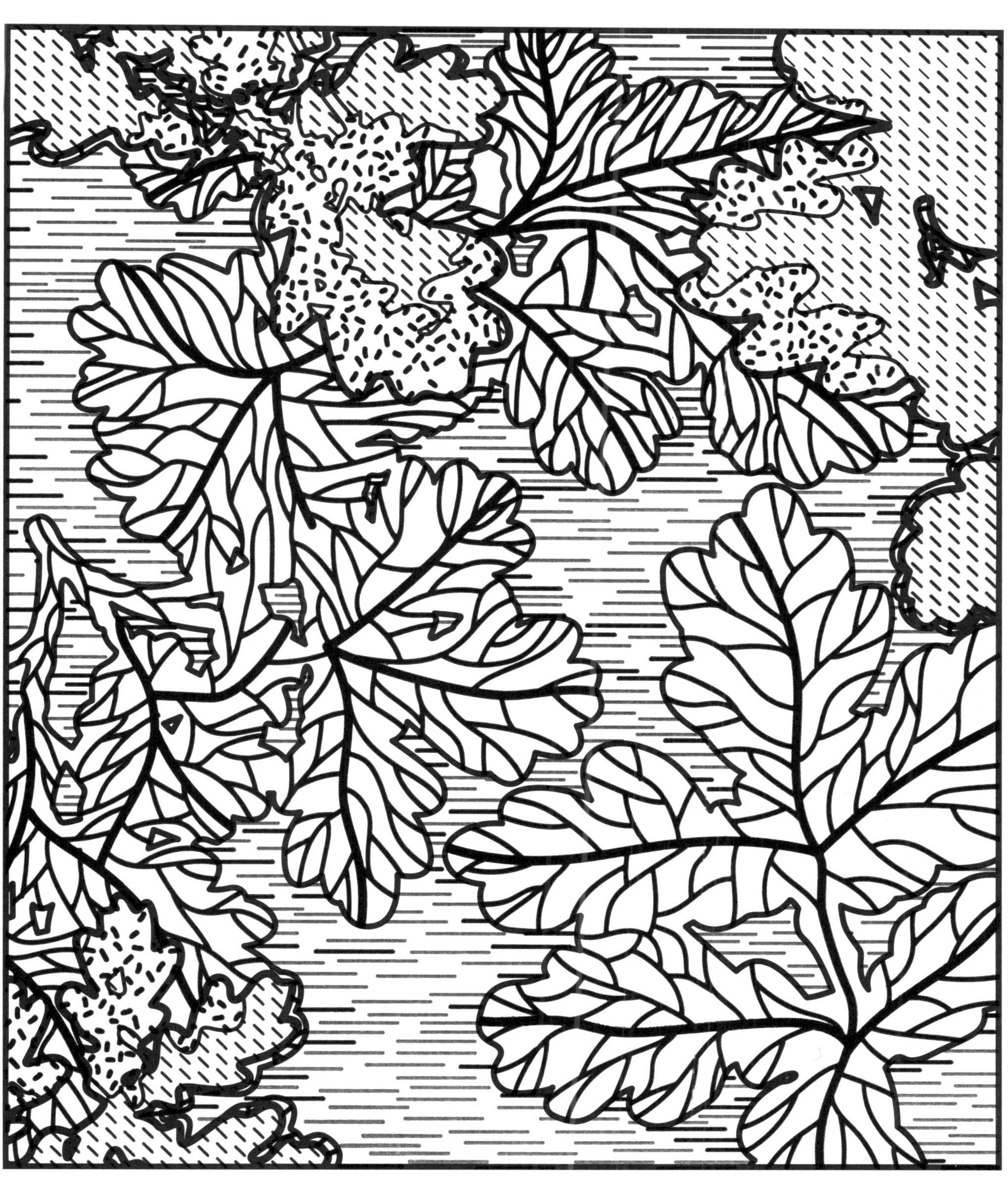

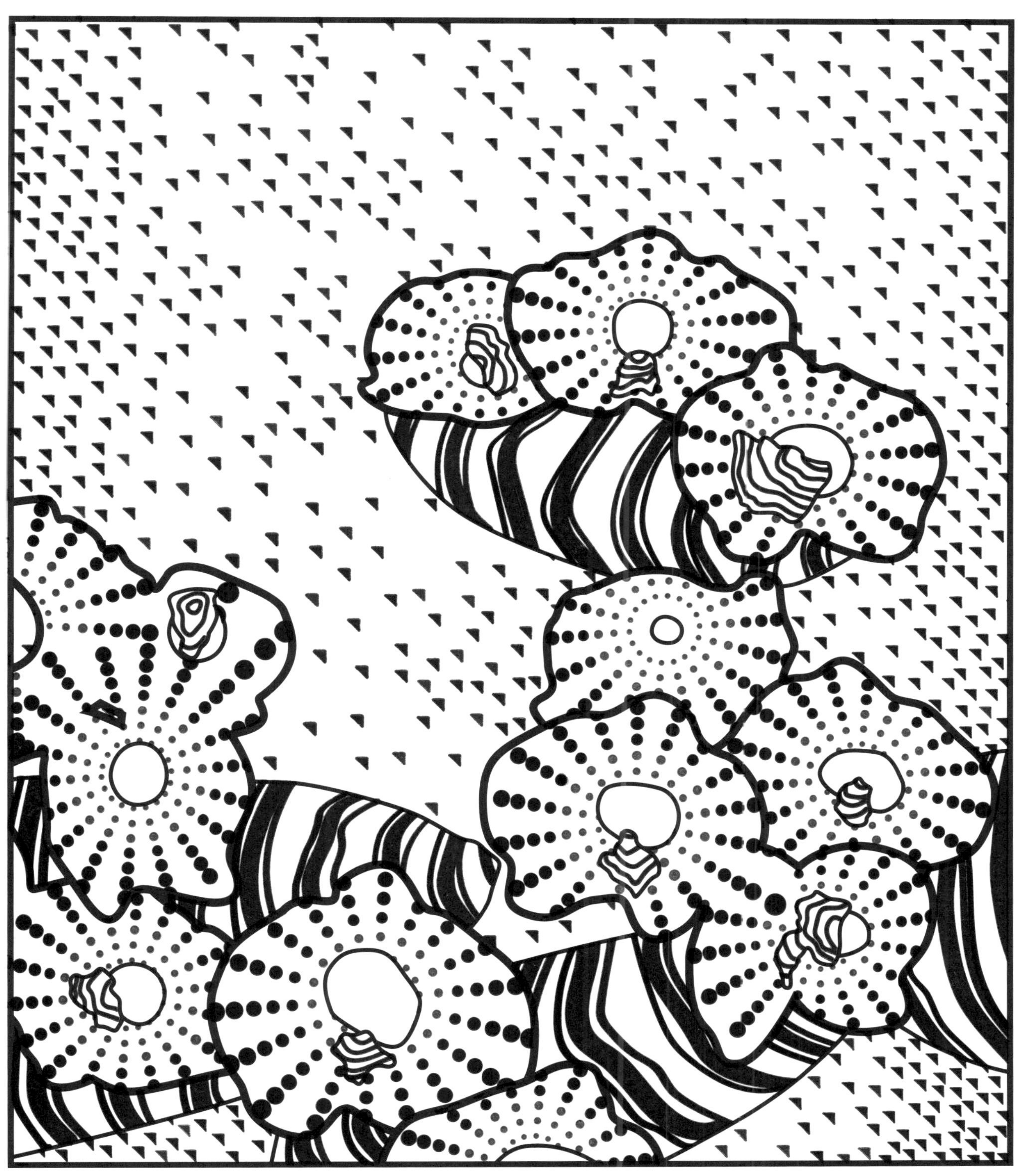

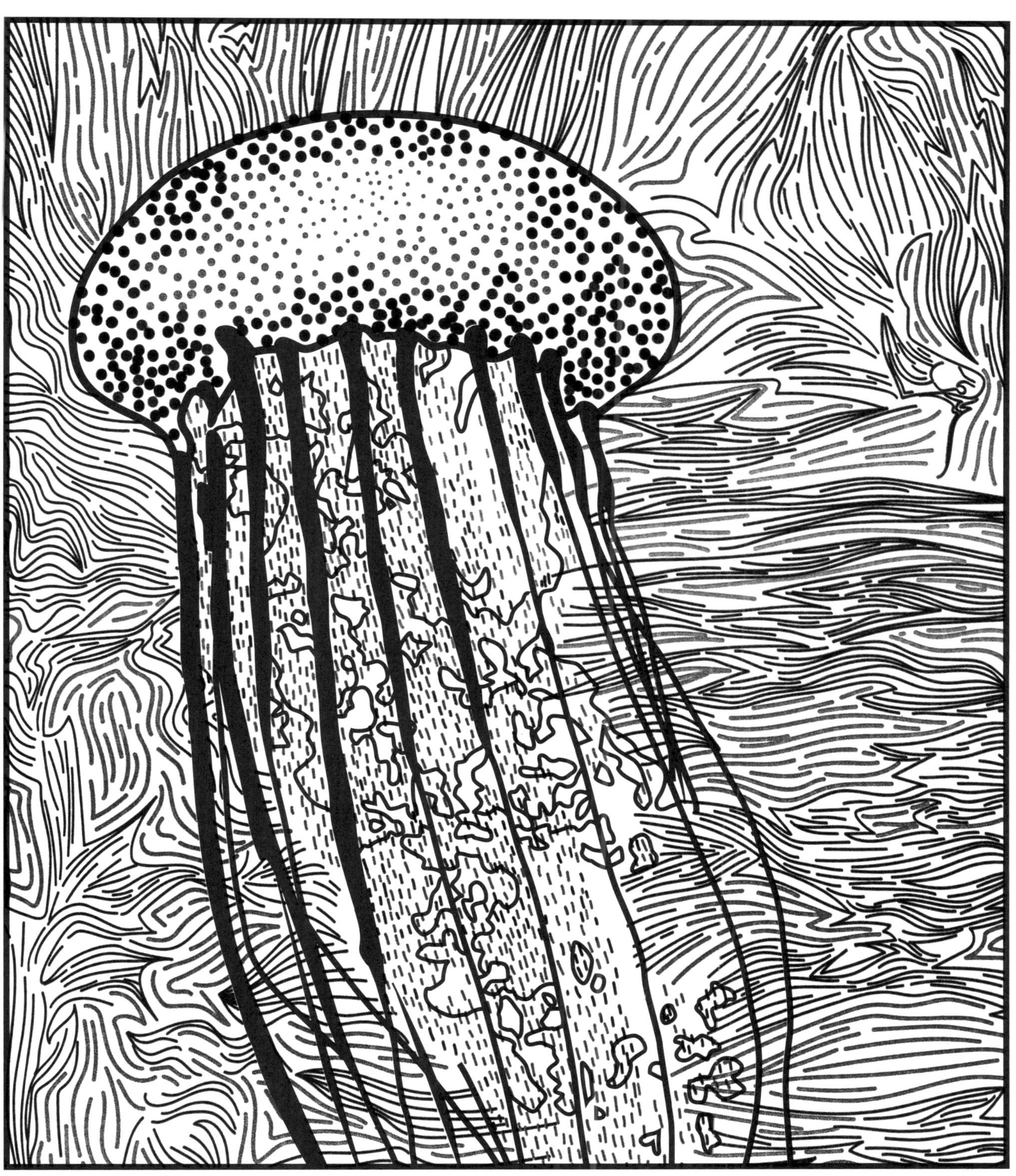

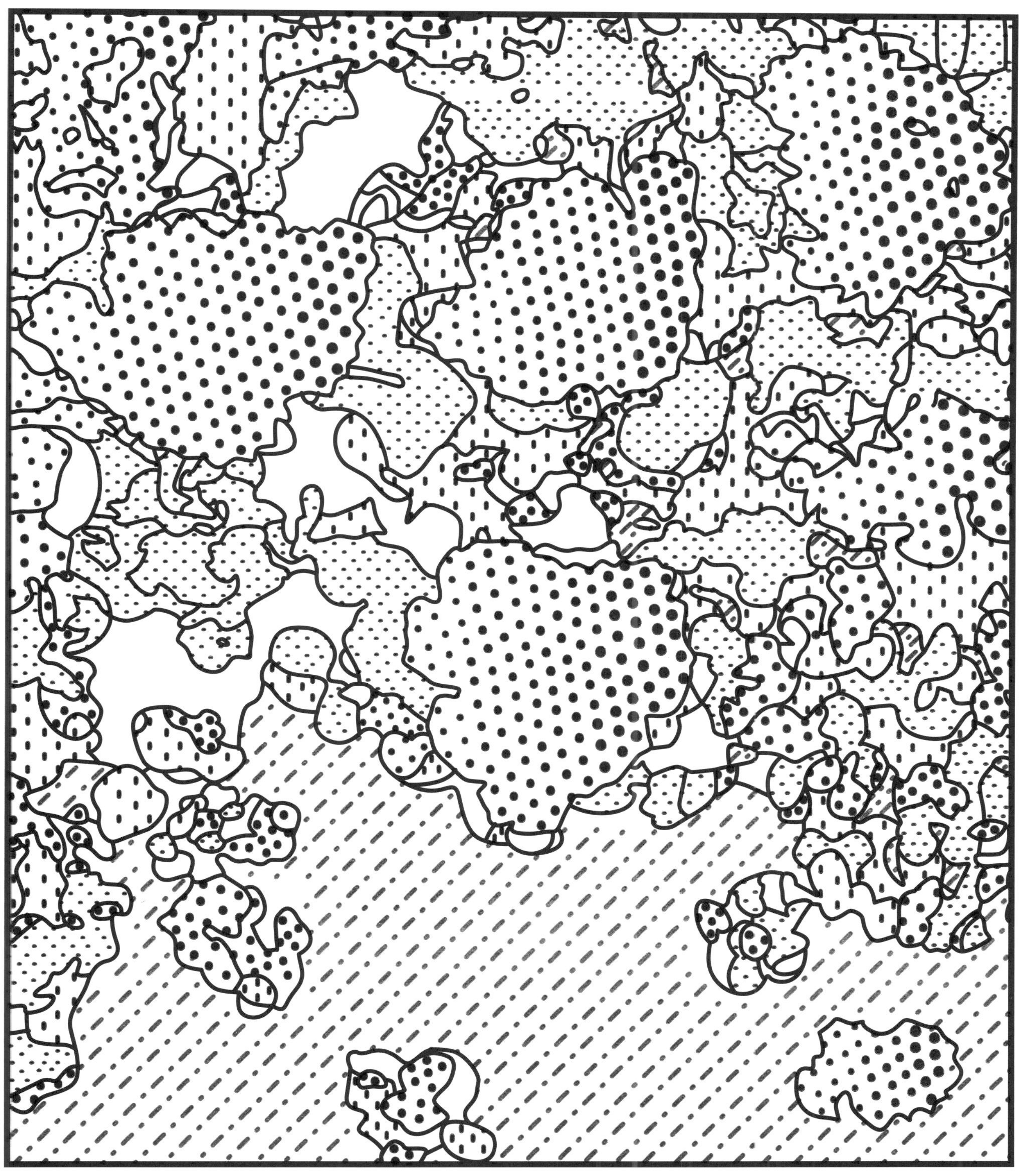

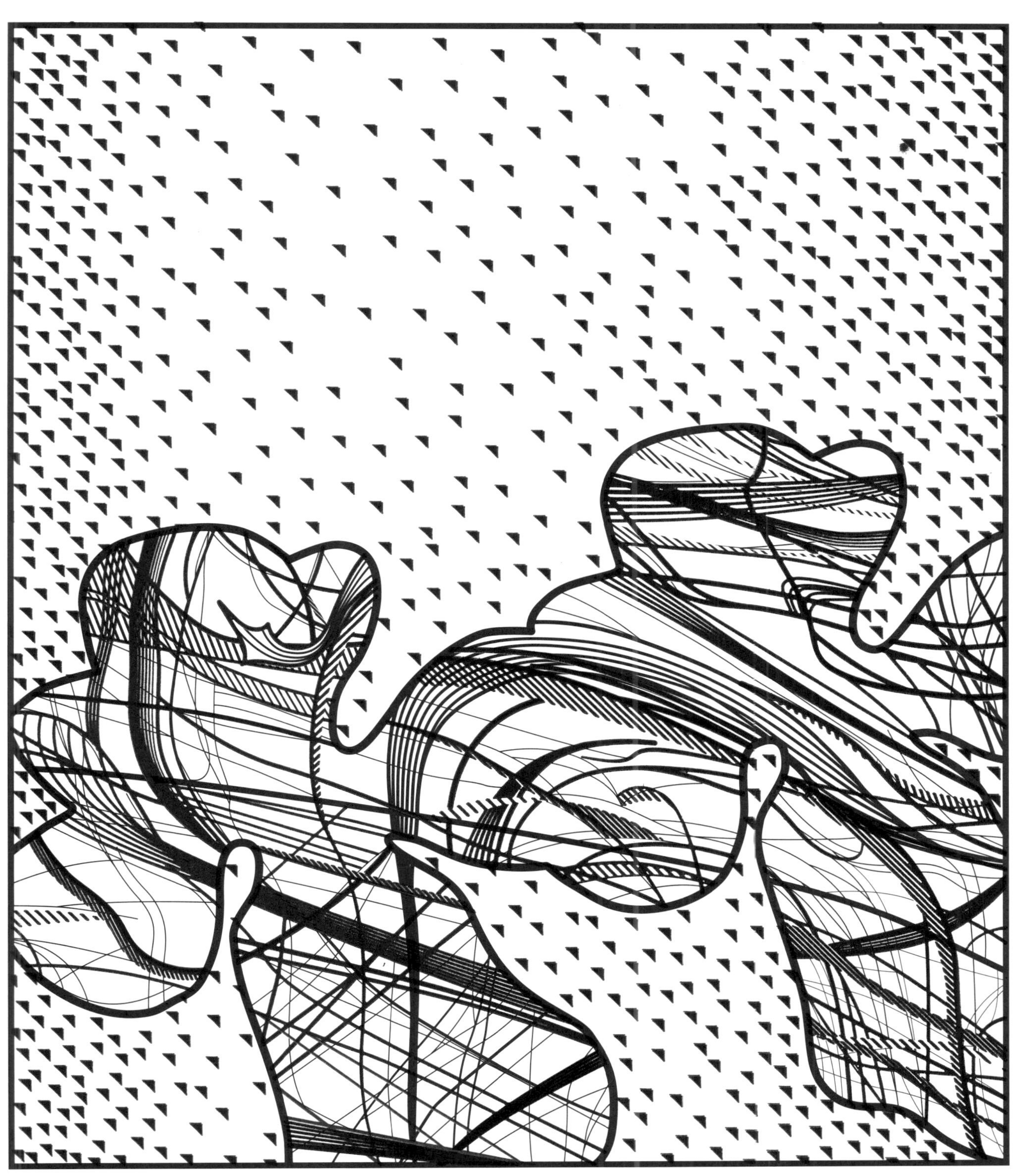

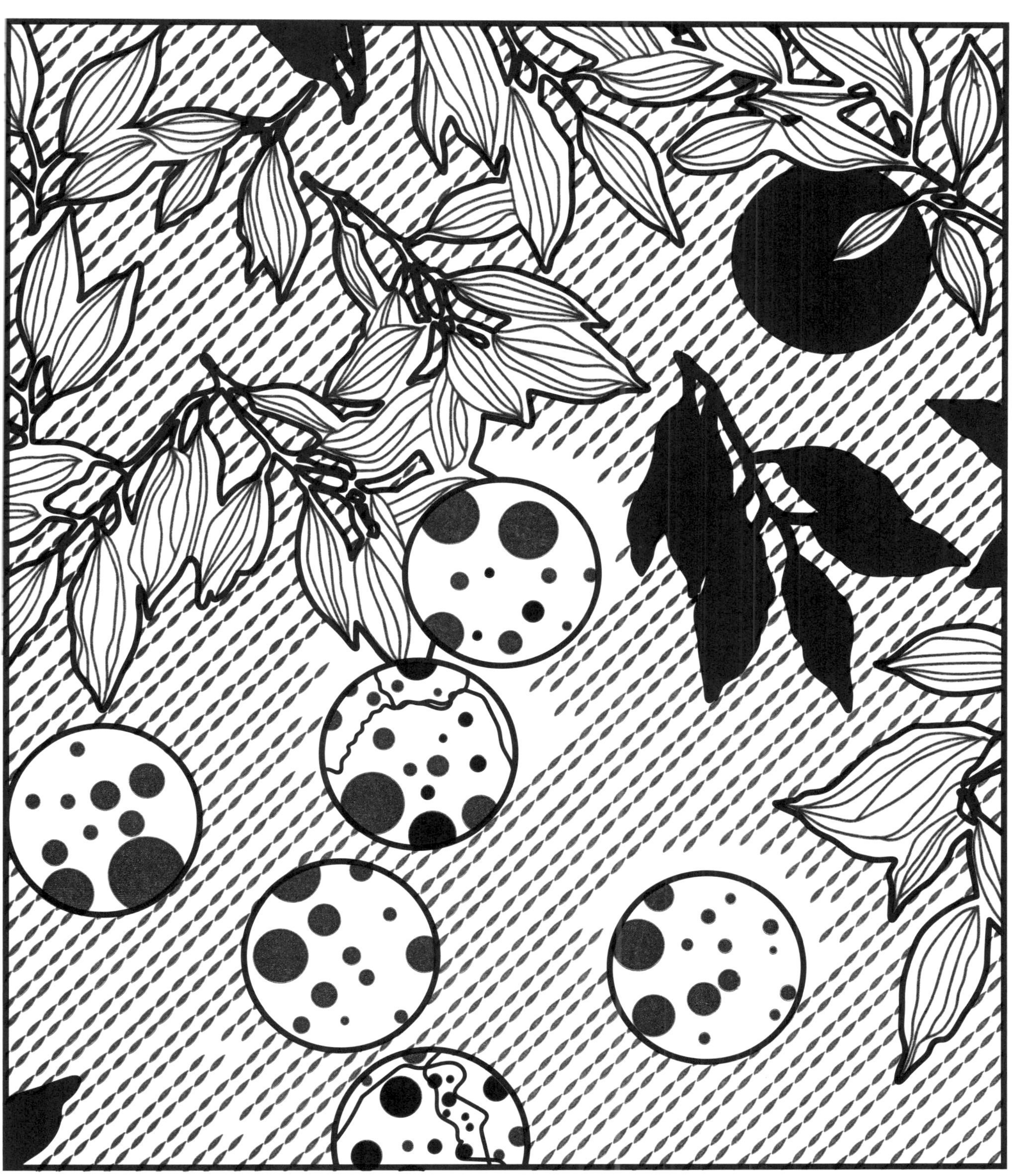

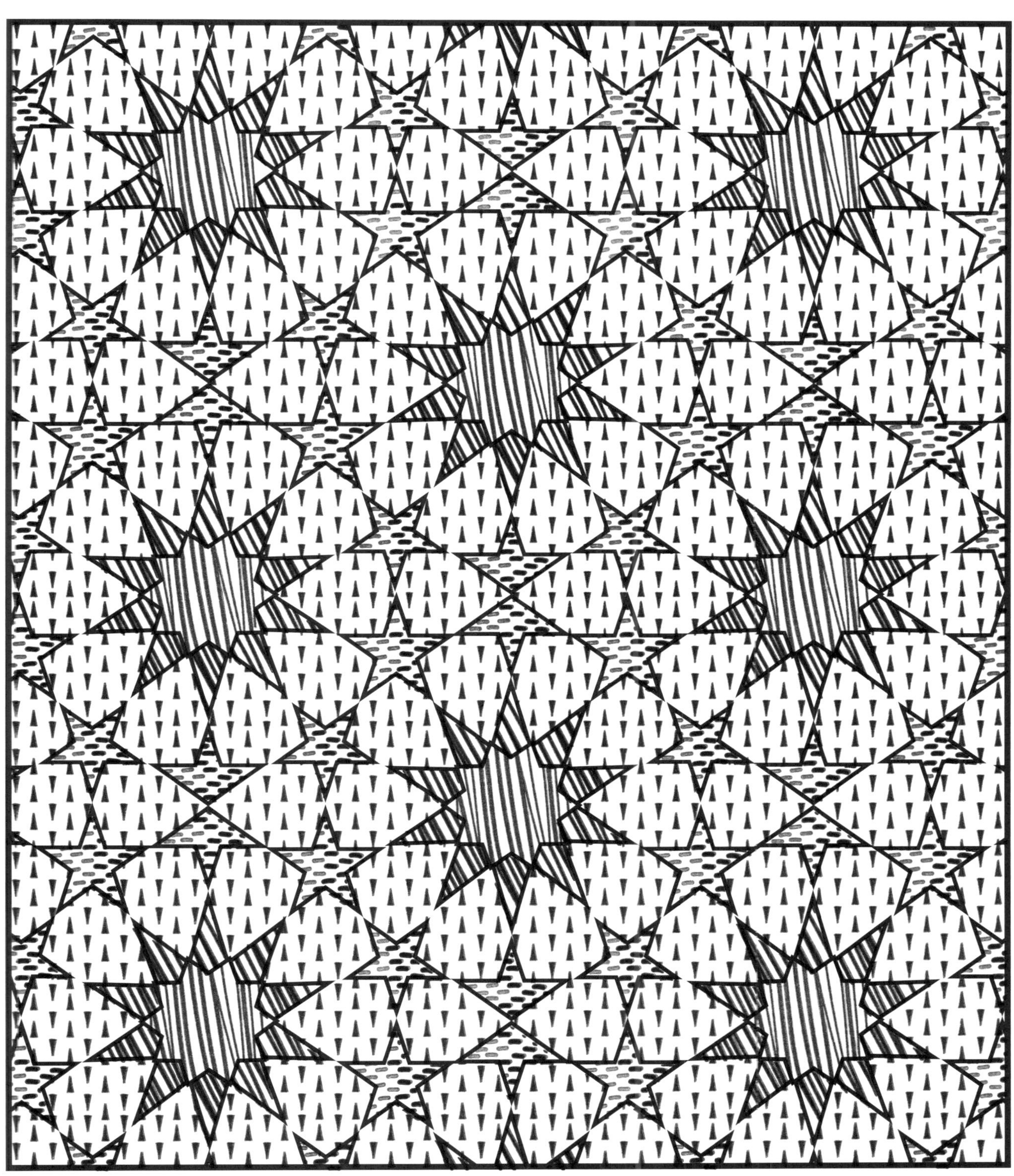

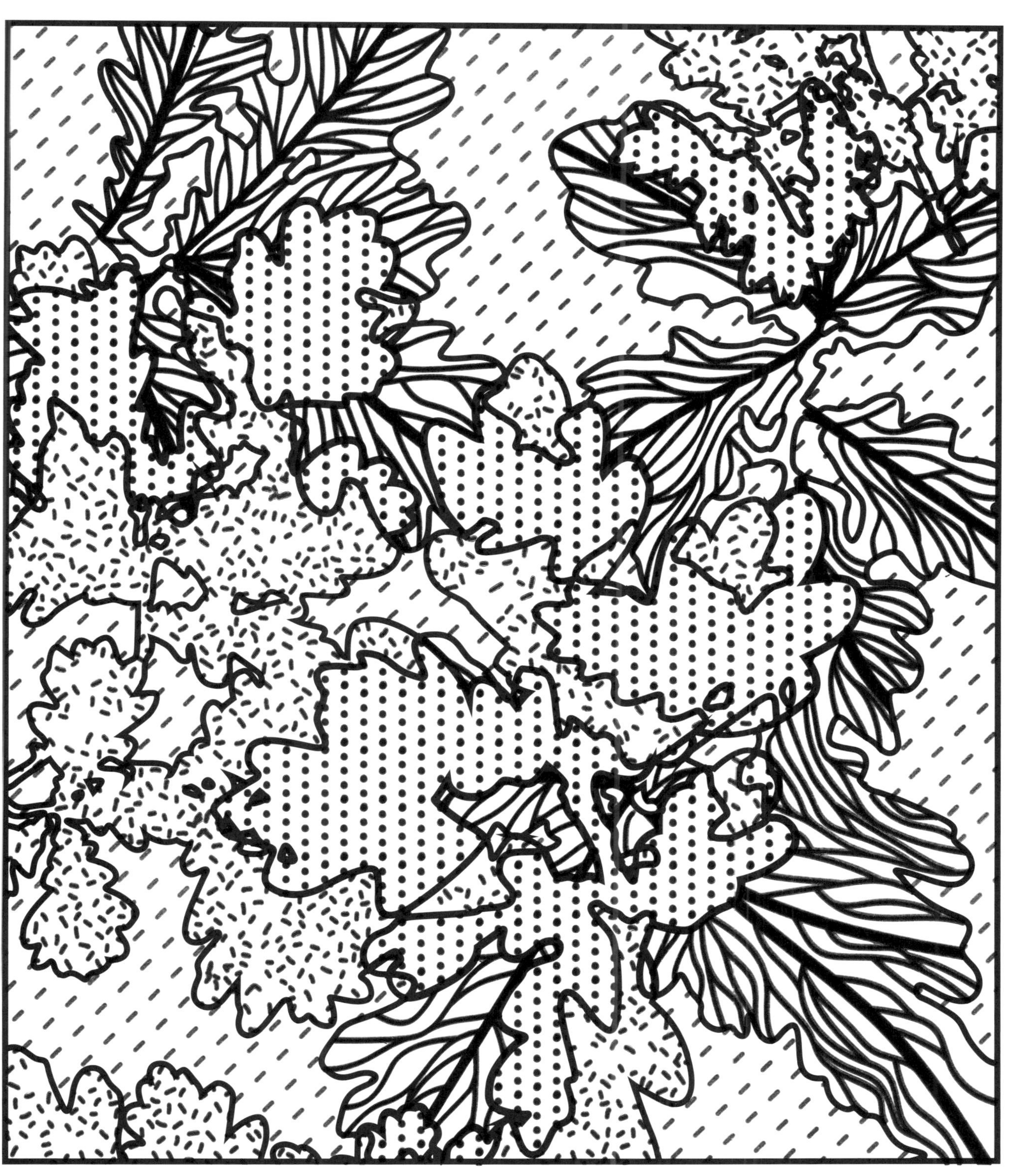

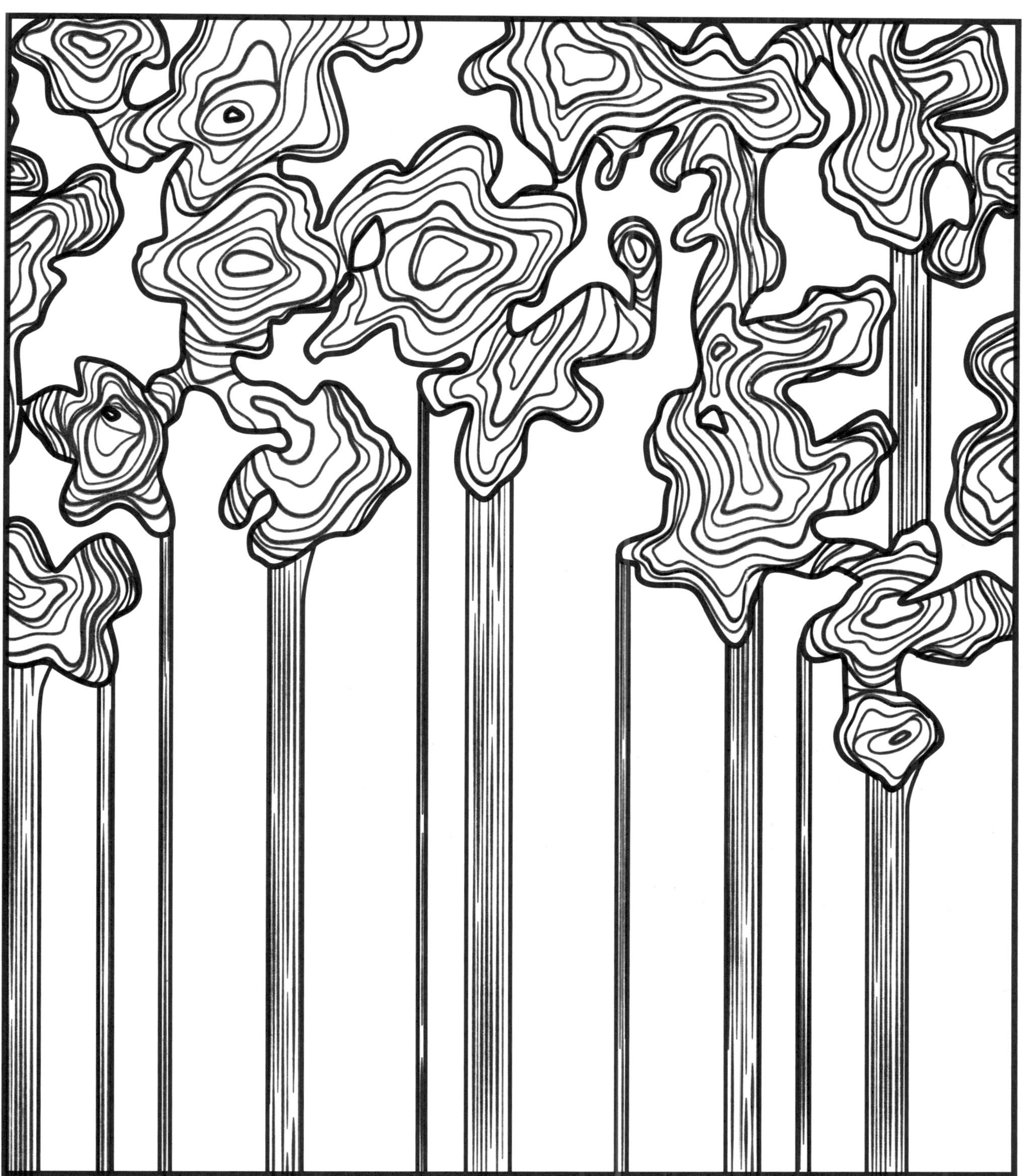